The 1992 Los Angeles Riots: The History of the Civil Disturbances across LA after the Beating of Rodney King

By Charles River Editors

A picture of National Guardsmen during the riots

About Charles River Editors

Charles River Editors is a boutique digital publishing company, specializing in bringing history back to life with educational and engaging books on a wide range of topics. Keep up to date with our new and free offerings with this 5 second sign up on our weekly mailing list, and visit Our Kindle Author Page to see other recently published Kindle titles.

We make these books for you and always want to know our readers' opinions, so we encourage you to leave reviews and look forward to publishing new and exciting titles each week.

Introduction

A picture taken by Ricky Bonilla during the riots

"I just want to say, you know, can we all get along?" – Rodney King

The fight for civil rights was at the forefront of inspirational, high-octane movements that took 20th century America by storm. It was a long time coming, to say the least, and yet, while some headway was made, progress was difficult and painfully slow. The historic advancements achieved during the Reconstruction Era were reversed by the Jim Crow law, a hideous set of statutes that enforced racial segregation. Although some of the most "progressive" northern states outwardly opposed those laws, black civilians and veterans alike who resided in these liberal states were still regarded as second-class citizens whose occupations were limited to farming, factory work, domestic service, and other low-wage jobs.

Time and again, black Americans had no choice but to take to the streets and demand their rights. It was only through the resilience of the black community, and the powerful, peaceful protests they mobilized that they were finally granted voting rights and equal employment opportunities as archaic segregation laws were formally dismantled. Sadly, not all Americans celebrated these momentous milestones for minorities, which were long overdue, and discrimination still reared its ugly head in many forms.

One of the most common complaints minorities had centered on the use of police brutality, an issue that remains at the forefront of the conversation today. While protests emerged after the death of George Floyd in 2020, perhaps the most notorious example of police brutality in modern American history was the beating of Rodney King, whose arrest was caught on video. The trial that followed and the acquittal of the police officers who attacked him touched off violence, much of which was captured on video and broadcast around the globe.

The 1992 Los Angeles Riots: The History of the Civil Disturbances across LA after the Beating of Rodney King examines the conditions and events that led to the riots, the damage done, and the aftermath. Along with pictures depicting important people, places, and events, you will learn about the LA riots like never before.

The 1992 Los Angeles Riots: The History of the Civil Disturbances across LA after the Beating of Rodney King

About Charles River Editors

Introduction

Tensions

Rodney King

Latasha Harlins

The Trial

The Riots

Online Resources

Further Reading

Free Books by Charles River Editors

Discounted Books by Charles River Editors

Tensions

"It's happening right now...it's just not on film, it's not being recorded." – Rodney King

On the surface, the 1980s and 1990s were an embodiment of a new, enlightened America, a colorful and united utopia of a nation that embraced diversity and propped up all of its citizens, regardless of race, gender, sexuality, or creed. The melanin in one's skin (or lack of), it seemed, was no longer a requisite for equal rights, nor did it determine the brightness of one's future.

Some of the most popular sitcoms and TV shows of these eras revolved around black families and featured predominantly black casts. Classics such as *The Jeffersons, Family Matters, The Fresh Prince of Bel-Air, Martin*, and *In Living Color* received consistently stellar ratings and were renewed for multiple seasons. In 1990, Miss USA crowned the first African-American winner, Carole Anne-Marie Gist, and in 1991, Sharon Pratt Kelly shattered two glass ceilings when she was elected mayor of the District of Columbia, becoming the first female and first African-American woman to preside over the capital.

This was the same year the iconic King of Pop released one of his most iconic singles, "Black or White," described by Epic Records as "a rock 'n' roll dance song about racial harmony." Not only was Michael Jackson a household name in the Land of the Free, he was a showstopping global sensation and remains one to this day, even in death (in 2020, Jackson topped the list of highest-paid deceased celebrities for the eighth consecutive year). Prince, Stevie Wonder, Diana Ross, Whitney Houston, and Lionel Richie were just some of the other black superstars who regularly topped the charts. Then, in 1992, Carol Moseley Braun became the first African-American woman elected to the US Senate and the first woman to triumph over an incumbent.

Outside of the limelight, however, minorities continued to battle thinly-veiled oppression and discrimination on a daily basis, and too many were incessantly failed by the justice system. The disproportionate number of African-Americans behind bars was nothing new, but black incarceration rates were steadily worsening. In 1984, the imprisonment rate for African-American males sat at 339 inmates per 100,000 residents, but by 1992, that number had swelled to 619. To put this in perspective, the incarceration rate of white males was 109 per 100,000. Minorities of all ages were subjected to racial profiling and police brutality, and this was only the tip of the iceberg.

It was virtually impossible to overcome the lopsided scales of justice, and in response to the explosive racial unrest that unfolded in the 1960s, President Richard

Nixon launched the infamous War on Drugs campaign in 1971, which implemented mandatory prison time for drug offenses. The Anti-Drug Abuse Act of 1986 set fixed minimum prison sentences for select drugs, which once again disproportionately affected minorities. For one, five grams of crack cocaine generated a minimum five-year sentence, yet the law was far more lenient with powder cocaine; the threshold for an identical sentence was 500 grams of "snow."

   Two years after the LA riots, John Ehrlichman, Nixon's White House counsel, admitted in an interview with *Harper* that the former president's drug crusade harbored a hidden agenda. He explained, "The...campaign...and the Nixon White House after that had two enemies: the anti-war left and black people...We knew we couldn't make it illegal to be either against the war or black, but by getting the public to associate the hippies with marijuana and blacks with heroin, and then criminalizing both heavily, we could disrupt those communities. We could arrest their leaders, raid their homes, break up their meetings, and vilify them night after night on the evening news. Did we know we were lying about the drugs? Of course we did."

   Of course, Nixon was not the first, nor was he the last president caught making derogatory comments about people of color. In a taped phone call to Nixon, President Reagan could be heard complaining about certain black delegates to the UN. "To see those monkeys from those African countries," Reagan told his predecessor. "Damn them, they're still uncomfortable wearing shoes!" Nixon responded to these foul remarks with a boisterous belly-laugh.

Throughout the 20th century, minorities and their allies staged a string of peaceful rallies and boycotts demanding an end to structural barriers and segregation and calling for judicial reform. The spectacular demonstrations spearheaded by activists like Claudette Colvin and Rosa Parks, the Little Rock Nine, the Greensboro Four, the Freedom Riders, and Martin Luther King, Jr. produced landmark changes, but in the grand scheme of things, the progress was often gradual if not sluggish. Lawmakers patted themselves on the back for achieving the bare minimum and making it possible for a fraction of non-white citizens to succeed. Meanwhile, too many poor minorities were still left in the lurch.

There were times when the deep-seated anger and desperation that arose from the administration's perpetuation of the same discriminatory system boiled over. Riots and mob violence, whether spontaneous or premeditated, often came about as a result, even as the motives of instigators and participants varied. Some were driven by emotion, typically a fervent opposition towards some perceived injustice in current affairs, while others were opportunists looking to capitalize on the chaos, namely through the theft of material items. Some of those wreaking havoc and inflicting brute violence upon strangers also took advantage of and contributed to the disarray to vent personal frustrations. Whatever the reasons, riots ultimately concluded with tragically avoidable losses.

In 1992, the City of Angels was transformed into a hellscape of fiery pandemonium and unchecked bloodshed in response to the notorious acquittal of four white police officers who were seen on videotape beating motorist Rodney King while arresting him. The five-day-long bedlam may not have been the longest or deadliest civil disturbances in American history, but the LA riots were the most financially crippling and among the most catastrophic of their kind to ever occur on US soil.

That said, those riots were hardly the first to be triggered by the abuse of police authority. As far back as May 4, 1886, labor leaders in Chicago organized a peaceful protest at Haymarket Square decrying the murder and wounding of numerous workers employed by the McCormick Reaper Works at the hands of police officers the previous day. The demonstration turned deadly when a protester lobbed a bomb at the police, killing seven policemen and four civilians, and maiming dozens of others. At the March on Washington 77 years later, demonstrators were still wielding placards bearing the same call for an end to police brutality.

The government, it seemed, was always aware of the alarming number of officers who were willing to abuse their authority. An excerpt from a document entitled "To Secure These Rights," penned by President Harry Truman's Committee on Civil Rights in 1947, noted, "We must...report more widespread and varied forms of official misconduct. These include violent physical attacks by police officers on [minorities]...There are other cases...of officers who seem to be 'trigger-happy.' In a number of instances, [blacks] have been shot, supposedly in self-defense, under circumstances indicating at best unsatisfactory police work, and at worst, a callous willingness to kill."

In fact, the 1992 riots did not mark the first time that Los Angeles locals rioted in response to police brutality. In 1965, mayhem erupted in the South Central neighborhood of Watts and engulfed adjacent neighborhoods over six days. By the time the smoke cleared, 34 civilians had died and property damage was priced at $40 million. The impetus was the arrest of 21-year-old Marquette Frye, who had been pulled over for drunk driving. A scuffle between Frye, his mother, brother, and the police ensued, culminating in the arrests of all three. Mobs formed when onlookers alerted the neighborhood that the police had assaulted and apprehended the Frye family, and some spread a rumor that two pregnant women had been kicked in the process. William Parker, then-chief of the Los Angeles Police Department (LAPD), ruffled more feathers when he later likened the rioters to "monkeys in a zoo."

By the start of the 1990s, Daryl Gates had been serving as chief of the LAPD for over a decade, and he was lauded in law enforcement circles for his initiative and glittering portfolio, which included accomplishments like founding the Drug Abuse Resistance Education (DARE) program. He was also responsible for certain innovations in the SWAT sector, which had been established in the 1960s to combat riots and strengthen the police force's response to violent confrontations with lawbreakers. Like many of his predecessors, however, he was also a divisive figure who had previously stoked the wrath of the public with some problematic comments. 10 years earlier, Gates made the following remark in an interview with the *LA Times,* for which he received bitter backlash: "We may be finding that in some blacks when [a chokehold] is applied, the veins or arteries do not open up as fast as they do in normal people."

Gates

Rodney King

"As a black man, you run from the cops. It's different now, but back when I was coming up, you run." – Rodney King

On the afternoon of March 2, 1991, a month shy of his 26th birthday, a black man by the name of Rodney King linked up with his friends Bryant "Pooh" Allen and Freddie Helms. They spent the day shooting the breeze while knocking back several 40-ounce bottles of Olde English 800 at another friend's residence. Around midnight, the inebriated trio stumbled into King's car, and King, whose blood alcohol level was double the legal limit, made the reckless decision to take the wheel and speed to a nearby liquor store. They reached their destination without incident, but after deciding they hadn't gotten enough alcohol, they tempted fate once more and embarked on a hunt for more.

King had just come off the freeway when he clocked the highway patrol cruiser on his tail. By then, it was roughly 40 minutes past midnight. As a parolee, the consequences of a DUI would have been twice as severe, and King, determined not to return to prison, floored it. A cacophony of sirens blared behind him as he veered around random corners, burning rubber at 80 mph in 35 mph speed zones. At one point, the speedometer got as high as 117 mph.

Eight miles later, the erratic vehicle finally grinded to a halt at the intersection of Osborne Street and Foothill Boulevard in Lake View Terrace, a normally quiet suburban neighborhood in San Fernando Valley. When King and his passengers exited the vehicle, they found themselves surrounded by a squadron of police cars, along with an LAPD chopper hovering overhead. The first LAPD officers on the scene were Theodore Briseno, Timothy Wind, Laurence Powell, Rolando Solano, and Sergeant Stacey Koon.

Koon

The three were commanded to lie flat on the ground and place their hands on their heads. By all witness accounts, Allen and Helms immediately did as they were told, but King's compliance left something to be desired so far as the cops were concerned. He was slow to follow orders, and he was seen playfully waving at the chopper. Melanie Singer, the highway patrol officer who initiated the pursuit, aimed her gun at King and reiterated the order. The suspect, she claimed, blew her a kiss and wiggled his rear at her in response. When he eventually dropped down on all fours, he failed to assume a prone position.

King's non-compliance turned slightly aggressive when the 6'3", 225-pound man shook the four officers attempting to clap irons on him. Koon zapped him twice with his taser, but the darts, packed with 50,000 volts each, had little effect. The officers later claimed that the combination of King's "spaced-out" expression and his volatile behavior led them to believe that he was "dusted," slang for being under the influence of PCP.

What happened next was taped by a local resident named George Holliday, who had slipped out to his patio to investigate the flashing lights and commotion outside his window. The beginning of the footage, which starts out blurry, shows King hoisting himself off the ground and attempting to run past Powell. Rather than tackle and cuff the unarmed suspect as soon as he was pinned to the ground, the camcorder, which slowly came into focus, recorded Officers Powell and Wind continuously and violently hitting him with their batons and kicking him.

The beating of King, who had already crumpled to the asphalt after the first clubbing, dragged on for about 80 seconds, during which the officers inflicted anywhere between 50 and 69 baton blows and kicks. Even worse, when the officers took a 10-second interlude, Briseno stepped on King's neck. In response, King squirmed under the weight of Briseno's foot, and another round of pummeling commenced. Briseno was also seen stomping on King's shoulder, causing the suspect's head to bang against the ground. Multiple blows and kicks were also directed at King's head, neck, and chest, which violated LAPD policy. None of the cops at the scene intervened, and all but one of the officers were white.

King was dropped off at the Pacifica Hospital, where he underwent a five-hour operation performed by three surgeons. Among his lengthy list of injuries were 11 skull fractures, broken bones and teeth, and kidney failure, and he suffered permanent brain damage and acute psychological trauma. There was a deep gash on the right cheek of King's swollen face, and his right eye was completely bloodshot.

On March 4, Holliday sold his tape to the local station *KTLA*, and it was broadcast that same evening. Unaware of the incriminating footage, the four arresting officers had grossly understated the violence they inflicted on King in their reports, who, according to them, had only sustained "cuts and bruises of a minor nature."

Perhaps not surprisingly, the video spread like wildfire. The following day, the video was aired repeatedly on just about every news station in America, so much so that Vice President Ed Turner of *CNN* called it "wallpaper." At the same time, the video shocked and enraged citizens across the country. A local poll revealed that 92% of LA residents believed that the officers had employed excessive force. At a conference held by the City Council, queues of civilians took the panel to task. One woman complained, "As a person of color, it is discomforting for me to be a target. I consider myself on an endangered species list." Even Gates, who defended his subordinates throughout the affair, had to acknowledge the inhumanity of their actions: "For the LAPD, considered by many the finest, most professional police department in the world, it was more than extreme. It was impossible."

Thanks to Holliday's video and mounting public pressure, King was released without charges, while Powell, Briseno, Wind, and Koon were indicted by a grand jury on March 15 and charged with excessive use of force and assault with a deadly weapon. Koon was also charged with aiding and abetting, and he and Powell received another charge for fabricating official reports.

Latasha Harlins

"Here on Earth, tell me what's a black life worth?

A bottle of juice is no excuse, the truth hurts." – Tupac Shakur

At 9:35 a.m. on the morning of March 16, 1991, just a day after the LAPD officers were indicted, a black 15-year-old named Latasha Harlins popped into the Empire

Liquor Market in Vermont Vista, a Korean-American-owned convenience store on her block. She grabbed a bottle of orange juice priced at $1.79, placed it in her backpack, fished two $1 bills out of her wallet, and headed towards the counter.

Soon Jadu, the 51-year-old woman behind the counter, was part-owner of the establishment, but she was not the regular cashier. She was temporarily manning the register for her husband, "Bill" Heung Ki Du, who was taking a nap in a van parked near the store. Soon later claimed that she had watched Harlins stuff the juice into her bag, and that she had missed the cash in the teenager's hand. As such, she called out to Harlins and accused her of shoplifting.

Harlins, in response, contested the allegation, and the exchange between the two quickly became heated. What happened next was caught on tape, this time via the store's security cameras. The physical confrontation began when Soon yanked at Harlins' jacket and hair. A brief tug-of-war for Harlins' backpack ensued, during which the teenager retaliated by swinging her backpack at the cashier and throwing two punches, hitting Soon square in the eye. Harlins' grip on the backpack was broken by the impact, and Soon, clutching the bag, toppled to the floor.

Soon sprung up from the floor and lobbed the backpack at Harlins. The teenager, looking away from Soon, adjusted her jacket and bent down to pick up the juice that had fallen out of her bag. The cashier simultaneously removed her .38-pistol from her holster. Harlins then placed the juice on the counter, only for Soon to swat the bottle aside. It was at this point that Harlins turned on her heel and began walking towards the door, while Soon cocked her pistol and shot Harlins point-blank in the back of her head.

Shortly after Harlins slumped to the ground, Soon's husband, who had heard the gunshot, rushed into the store. The hysterical Soon screamed that they had been robbed before passing out. He then called the cops, reporting a "hold-up," claiming that the thief had been "taking...money out of the register," and that the "robber lady" had been shot.

The city's grief, compounded by Harlins' tragic death, was still raw when, on March 21, all four officers involved in the King incident pleaded not guilty. Nine days later, Tom Bradley – the first and only black mayor of Los Angeles, established the Christopher Commission alongside the task force's namesake, Warren Christopher, who had previously served as the US Deputy Secretary of State. After a three-month-long inquiry into the department's operations, the commission compiled a report that exposed a multi-generational culture of racial discrimination and overt abuse of power within the LAPD, while further documenting countless cases that were swept under the rug by police officers. Among the various revelations the commission uncovered was a secret code that many officers used in reference to disturbances in the black neighborhoods of South LA: "NHI," an acronym for "No Humans Involved." Furthermore, law enforcement officials of all ranks were caught describing the African-Americans they had sworn to protect and serve as "monkeys" and "gorillas." The use of other notorious epithets was routine for many.

Bradley

Christopher

Indeed, a transcript of the radio transmissions sent during the night of King's beating indicated that this was, for at least one of the officers, not an isolated incident. Powell was heard describing another domestic disturbance, also involving African-Americans, as "right out of *Gorillas in the Mist*." To this, the foot patrol laughed and replied, "Let me guess who be the parties." At 1:13 a.m., Powell gloated to the foot patrol, "I haven't beaten anyone this bad in a long time."

Given the damning video evidence, for the jury at Soon's trial, it was an open-and-shut case. On October 2, 1991, they found Soon guilty of voluntary manslaughter and recommended a 10-year term. Nonetheless, on the day of sentencing, Judge Joyce Karlin commuted Soon's sentence to five years of probation and 400 hours of community service, and the judge ordered the defendant to pay $500 in restitution and funeral expenses. Karlin's reasoning was that Soon had an otherwise clean record and that her actions were products of the mental scars she sustained from past robberies.

Harlins' family and supporters were understandably crushed by Karlin's decision. Not only was the jury's recommendation less than the maximum penalty (16 years), Soon would not be spending a single second behind bars. Objectors pointed to another recent case, wherein a teenager received the full 16-year term for accidentally shooting and killing his friend during a prom night. More egregious yet was the story of Korean-American defendant named Brendan Sheen, who was jailed for a month for his kicking his dog. "She...had her whole life ahead of her," Harlins' cousin Shinese lamented. "She just knew her dreams and her goals...But unfortunately she didn't make it to her dreams. She wasn't a thief. She died with $2 in her hand."

Tensions between the African-American and Korean-American communities in LA had always existed, but they deteriorated further in the months following Harlins' death. In late May, two Korean-American employees at a liquor store near 35th Street and Central Avenue were gunned down by black robbers even after submitting to their demands. Shortly after, on June 4, Tae Sam Park, proprietor of Chung's Liquor Market, shot a black patron named Arthur Mitchell five times in the chest during what was allegedly a botched hold-up. Mitchell had apparently attempted to settle the remaining 25-cent balance for a wine cooler with a piece of jewelry. When Park's wife declined to make the sale, Mitchell joined her behind the counter, where he reached into his pocket, jabbed it in her direction as if he was holding a pistol, and demanded the contents of the register. Unlike the Harlins and King cases, there was no footage of the incident, and the only witnesses were the employers and employees of the establishment. The police, who concluded that Park had acted in self-defense, opted against pressing charges. Two other Korean-American shopkeepers killed black civilians between April and October.

Black protesters camped outside Soon's courtroom and the Korean-owned establishments. "Don't shop where you can't work" one banner read. "We will not shop with killers," read another. "No justice, no peace," the crowds cried. "Boycott Korean!"

Alongside the peaceful demonstrations led by the National Urban League, the Brotherhood Crusade, and the Bethel African Methodist Episcopal Church, the frictions continued to escalate in small, yet dangerous bursts. On November 26, 1991, Molotov cocktails were hurled into Ace Liquor Store. 19 days later, a group busted the windows of nine parked cars at a Korean Catholic church. Several other Korean businesses fell victim to vandalism.

The Trial

"The failure to control these officers is a management issue that is at the heart of the problem. The documents and data that we have analyzed have all been available to the department; indeed, most of this information came from that source. The LAPD's failure to analyze and act upon these revealing data evidences a significant breakdown in the management and leadership of the Department. The Los Angeles Board of Police Commissioners, lacking investigators or other resources, failed in its duty to monitor the Department in this sensitive use of force area. The Department not only failed to deal with the problem group of officers but it often rewarded them with positive evaluations and promotions." – excerpt from the Christopher Commission's findings

On the same day of the Ace Liquor Store firebombing, 11 days after the judge's decision in the Soon case, the officers' lawyers successfully convinced the court to move the trial to Simi Valley, a majority-white suburb in Ventura County. Their attorneys contended that there was no way a trial without "bias" could be conducted in LA on account of the high-profile nature of the case. Superior Court Judge Bernard Kamins was removed from the case, supposedly for telling the District Attorney not to "panic," and that he could "trust [him]." His replacement was Judge Stanley Weisberg, who had been criticized for previous controversial rulings. The prospect of a venue change had always been on the horizon, but the relocation and the court's choice of judge led the plaintiff's supporters to complain. Roger Gunson, Chief Deputy of the Special Investigations Division in the District Attorney's office, remarked, "I have never been so horrified in my life."

The prosecutors' fears heightened when the jury was assembled. Of the 12 selected, nine were white, one was biracial, one was Asian, and one was Hispanic. Background checks determined that all jurors were ardent advocates of law enforcement. Moreover, two were veterans, and two others belonged to the NRA. Chief

Prosecutor Terry White protested, "They all seemed to come from the same background." The defense team's jury consultant, Jo-Ann Dimitrius, called them a "gem of a jury."

Following the delivery of his opening statement on March 5, 1992, White rolled the Holliday tape on the big screen. The video, which was replayed multiple times throughout the trial, was paramount in the prosecution's case.

Despite the footage, the officers claimed that King had lunged at Powell. The defense attorneys claimed that King alone was "in control of the situation" and identified him as the sole aggressor. Conversely, Briseno's attorney pinned the blame on Powell in a bid to distance his client from culpability. Briseno formally denounced his colleagues' actions, characterizing Powell as "out of control." The only reason he stepped on King's neck, he insisted, was to keep the other officers at bay, for they were "doing things that didn't make any sense."

Singer was the only officer aside from the indicted four officers to take the stand. She testified that she was tempted to tend to King's injuries, but that she was thwarted by her fear of being mocked by her associates. She explained, "I didn't want those guys to start heckling me...There is no doubt in my mind that [Powell] struck [King] in the face. I will never forget it to the day I die.”

King's side of the story was vivid. His attempt to make a run for it, as demonstrated in the tape, was prompted, he claimed, by a chilling threat. He claimed that the cops told him, “We're going to kill you, [n-word]. Run!” “I felt beat up and like a crushed can,” said King. “That's what I felt like, like a crushed can all over, and my spirits were down real low.” When it came to the Holliday video, however, most of the dialogue during the encounter was drowned out by distance and the roar of the chopper's rotor blades, so the contents of the verbal exchanges that transpired could only be gleaned from the conflicting testimonies.

To many outsiders, it may have seemed that the prosecution’s case was solid and that convictions were certain. Local black citizens, on the other hand, were intimately familiar with the unfairness of the justice system and braced for the worst, and their fears were proven right. On April 29, 1992, the day of the verdict, supporters on both sides paced outside the East County Courthouse with bated breath. When the defendants arrived, well-wishers showered them with donuts, other gifts, and words of encouragement. Koon, dressed in a floral-printed Hawaiian shirt, looked to be in a jovial mood. He swung his hands side-to-side as he walked towards the lobby, asked reporters about the ballgame the day before, and engaged in idle chit-chat.

At 3:10 p.m., the clerk announced the verdicts. All four officers were acquitted of 10 of the 11 counts. Five of the jurors had fought to make the charge of excessive force on Powell stick, but they were ultimately unable to sway the others, ending in a hung jury on that charge.

The disillusionment and despair of the public was immediately palpable. USC criminal law professor Jody Armour recounted the dismay that rippled across the country: "My jaw dropped. There was ocular proof of what happened...And yet, we saw a verdict that told us we couldn't trust our lying eyes..."

Armour's sentiments were echoed by various politicians and public figures across the country. One of the most poignant statements was issued by Mayor Bradley, who took to the podium at approximately 4:58 p.m. and appeared visibly shaken. "Today, this jury told the world that what we all saw with our own eyes wasn't a crime," Bradley declared. "Today, that jury asked us to accept the senseless and brutal beating of a helpless man...My friends, I am here to tell this jury: no. No, our eyes did not deceive us...what we saw was a crime. The jury's verdict will never blind the world to what we saw on the videotape."

Fully aware of the resentment and escalating discord that had been brewing in the streets of LA, Bradley urged listeners to keep the peace: "We must not endanger the reforms we have achieved by resorting to mindless acts. We must not push back progress by striking back blindly." Ira Reiner from the LA District Attorney's office concurred: "We disagree with the jury, but are obliged to accept the integrity of that verdict. It's a time for sober reflection, not recrimination." President George Bush, Sr. himself chimed in, saying, "What's needed now is calm, respect for the law."

Ultimately, the pleas would fall on deaf ears.

The Riots

"First you didn't give a f***, but you're learnin' now

If you don't respect the town then we'll burn you down."
– Tupac Shakur

The emotionally-charged tumult outside the Ventura County Superior Courthouse was merely a taste of what was coming. While those on both sides started trading insults with each other and Wind and Koon received a scathing earful from the demonstrators, motorists along Normandie Avenue pounded on their car horns in protest. Civilians began to spew obscenities at random cops patrolling the streets, and Powell was pelted with stones on the way to his car.

Aside from the 300 protesters who had assembled outside the courthouse within an hour of the verdict's delivery, more peaceful protesters arrived at the First AME Church to listen to rousing speeches aimed at strengthening the hurting community's resolve. Some wept inconsolably, while others linked arms and bowed their heads in prayer. By the evening's end, the church was hosting a diverse crowd of about 2,000, and Reverend Cecil Murray addressed the sea of faces before him from the pulpit. Like other leaders across the nation, the reverend lambasted the jury's failure to convict the men who perpetrated and allowed the "brutalization of an unarmed, prostrate man." He also entreated the public not to descend to the level of the attackers, but to take civic action instead. "Be cool," the reverend implored them. "Even in anger, be cool...If you're gonna burn something down, don't burn down the house of the victims, brother! Burn down the Legislature! Burn down the courtroom! Burn it down by voting, brother! Burn it down by standing with us at Parker Center! Burn it down by saying to Daryl Gates: 'This far, and no farther!'"

Meanwhile, another pack of peaceful protesters convened at the Hansen Dam Recreation & Sports Complex, which was situated near the site of King's beating and arrest. They, too, leaned on one another for solace and shared in the anguish, trying to make sense of the verdicts. Together, they marched towards the Foothill Division headquarters of the LAPD and resumed their rally there.

However, as earnest and urgent as the protest leaders' appeals for calm were, the start of the impending riots took place roughly 50 minutes after the verdicts were announced when a group of youths ruptured the padlock and shattered the windows of Tom's Liquor Store, owned by Korean-American Simon Choi, on 1355 W-Florence Avenue. About 100 self-serving individuals stormed into the premises and made off with 100 cases of malt liquor bottles, 90 malt liquor cans, and an assortment of other merchandise. The wares that were left were smashed to bits, and even when the store had been picked clean, looters continued to rummage through the toppled shelves, the soles of their shoes crunching on glass shards and adhering to the sticky floors caked in dried booze. Tom's Liquor, now "Tom's Market," was the first of some 200 liquor stores that would be looted over the next few days.

Three blocks away from the Florence and Dalton junction, five black men walked into the Korean-owned Payless Liquor and Deli and swiped 24 bottles of Olde English 800. When David Lee, the shopkeeper's son, confronted the thieves, one of them struck him in the head with a bottle. "This is for Rodney King!" yelled the assailant. Two of his accomplices flung bottles at the glass door, which burst into pieces. The same message was later spray-painted onto the charred walls of other spirit shops.

Throughout the riots, it was clear that the LAPD, from beat cops to high-ranking veterans, was unprepared for a civil disturbance of this magnitude, which the department handled with a mix of abject inadequacy and overzealousness. In the words of City Councilman Zev Yaroslavvsky, the riots were the "Pearl Harbor of the LAPD."

The department also received a spate of reports regarding individuals who were battering the windows of random cars. Officers Ty Hansen and John Ayala responded to one such report that a suspect, a black man with a buzz cut and a goatee, was going to town on the windshield of a Cadillac, occupied by a pair of white passengers, with an aluminum bat. Onlookers were unfazed, and some were actually cheering him on.

When police appeared on the scene, the bat-toting suspect booked it and led the cops on a foot-chase. Two other black officers, answering their colleagues' call for back-up, joined the pursuit. They eventually cornered the suspect in an alley regularly haunted by the Eight Tray

Gangster Crips. The ruckus also drew a throng of spectators, along with a camera crew, who booed and jeered at the officers as they cuffed the suspect while chanting King's name.

"What you gonna do, beat me?" a man taunted Ricky Banks, a black cop.

"You sold out to the white man, Uncle Tom," snarled another.

Sergeant Don Schwartzer described the scene: "It got ugly...We were the friendly neighborhood cops one minute, the next minute we were lunch meat. It didn't take a genius to figure out we needed to do something...We got out of there."

At 5:34 p.m., 35 cops rushed to the intersection of Florence and Normandie, frequently dubbed the "epicenter" of the riots, to disperse an unruly crowd that was slinging beer cans and rocks at passing vehicles. Two black officers caught and apprehended 16-year-old Seandal Daniels, who had reportedly chucked rocks at several squad cars. The 100 or so residents who had poured out into the yard chastised the officers for slamming the teenager onto the ground, prompting the gurgling Daniels to utter, "I can't breathe." When Sergeant Sam Arase shoved the teenager into the back of their cruiser, the agitated crowd began throwing rocks, bottles, and other projectiles at the vehicle.

Rachel Hindman's picture of the intersection

The responding officers were overwhelmed by the furor that surrounded them. "[There seemed to be] millions of people, not only in the sidewalk, but in the middle of the street," Arase recalled. Four helicopters – one police chopper and three deployed by local news stations – only magnified the confusion.

Meanwhile, the bulk of the 35 officers spotted camcorders in the hands of two black bystanders, and quickly became camera-shy. Rather than lock arms and fend off the protesters with their batons, as per crowd-control protocol, most made zero attempts to intervene, and a handful tried to verbally placate the mob, to no avail. It was Lieutenant Michael Moulin who made the contentious call to vacate the scene. "Forget the flashlight, it's not worth it," Moulin commanded his subordinates through his megaphone. "It ain't worth it. Let's go."

Several of Moulin's colleagues back at the precinct took issue with the abrupt retreat, which they chalked up to cowardice. Defending the order, Moulin cited the officers' vulnerability, pointing out that they were not equipped with any protective gear and may have had to rely on their firearms to stave off the mob, which would have likely resulted in deaths. Regardless, from that point forward, the police presence would become increasingly scarce.

By 6:30 p.m., another swarm of demonstrators had flocked to Parker Center, the LAPD headquarters. Chief Gates emerged shortly thereafter and hastily assured the crowd that the department would handle the matter "calmly, maturely, and professionally" before ducking into his car and backing out of the driveway. A fundraiser for the opposition of Charter Amendment F, which sought to curtail the police chief's power in favor of City Hall and initiate more civilian investigations on officer misconduct, awaited him in Brentwood.

Predictably, the crowd at Parker Center became incensed by the department's inaction and seeming indifference, and once again, the situation escalated. One man splashed gasoline on a parking kiosk and struck a match, making it one of the first structures to be destroyed by fire during the riots.

Why Gates refused to cancel his appearance at the gala and tend to what was obviously a far more pressing matter remains a subject of debate. Some say his apathy may have stemmed from arrogance - in a recent interview, Gates asserted that those who had learned from the Watts Riot "[realized] it would be total insanity to do that again." Still, if another insurrection of a similar scale were to arise, the LAPD, he declared, "would stop it the first night." Clearly, Gates was sorely mistaken on multiple levels – not only did people of all backgrounds participate in the rioting, the cops failed to deescalate the riot without external help, much less on the first night.

Similar scenes of chaos unfolded at City Hall two blocks away. One man in mustard-yellow pants was photographed climbing onto the hood of a Jaguar and stomping on the windshield as onlookers spurred him on. A fire was also kindled in the lobby, but the flames were swiftly smothered by nearby staff members.

Back at Florence and Normandie, the restless civilians who spooked Moulin and his men became more emboldened by the continued absence of law enforcement. As seen in footage recorded by news choppers and amateur cameramen, truculent rioters egged those around them to "get the Buddha heads and white boys." Footage captured some telling "Mexican m*********** to get the f*** out of their neighborhood."

Hapless civilians in the area, many of whom matched these "descriptions," were waylaid, mugged, and beaten to varying degrees. Bart Bartholomew, a white photographer for *The New York Times*, was one of these victims. He was blindsided by a wooden plank that cracked his jaw open and roughed up further by other rioters who snatched his camera and slugged him several times over. Luckily, a black Air Force veteran named Timothy Goldman heeded his cries for help and whisked him off to safety.

Absent the police, media members were forced to fill in for authorities. Department procedures dictated that locations of active riots be cordoned off immediately, but given the fact that the cops were a no-show, the burden of warning the public to clear the area fell upon the shoulders of radio stations and the media helicopters above. Some people who had no access to the reports or had simply turned off these mediums of communication strayed into the belly of the beast.

At 6:43 p.m., Larry Tarvin drove down Florence and stopped at a red light at Normandie. Since the delivery truck he was operating, stocked with medical supplies on the way to Chile, had no radio, he was oblivious to the ongoing riot and had not even learned about the exonerations of King's assailants. Suddenly, a man on the corner, who seemed to be pointing right at him, caught his eye. "Next thing I knew," said Tarvin. "There was something flying through the windshield."

A gang of rioters, among them Henry Watson, circled the truck and dragged Tarvin out of the cabin. They subsequently took turns pummeling Tarvin, who was curled into a defenseless ball on the ground, and kicking his head. Next, one of the attackers grabbed a fire extinguisher from the truck and bashed him over the head. Tarvin was knocked out for over a minute, but he eventually managed to summon enough energy to peel himself off the road.

"Enough is enough!" Tarvin yelled at the looters who were helping themselves to the truck's cargo. His attackers descended upon him once more. "No pity for the white man," said one of them. "Now you know how Rodney King felt, white boy."

Then, as quickly as the attack began, Tarvin's savior appeared. A black man repelled Tarvin's assailants, heaved the grievously injured man back into the truck's cabin, and dropped him off at the closest hospital. Despite Tarvin's best efforts, his quest to unveil his savior's identity, whose first name, ironically, was Rodney, was futile.

Just three minutes after the attack on Tarvin, Reginald Denny, a truck driver for Transit Mixed Concrete Co., unwittingly rolled into the lawless intersection in his 18-wheeler. When he finally noticed the looters emptying the contents of Tarvin's abnormally parked truck, it was too late. Of course, the thought of turning back around occurred to him, but the enormous vehicle's restrictive steering capabilities prevented him from doing so. As such, Denny convinced himself that the looters would have no interest in the 27 tons of sand in his truck, thus permitting him to "tiptoe across [the] intersection and get on down the road."

Denny's instincts were misguided. The looters hit the driver's window with rocks, and unlike Tarvin, whose memory of the attack was marked by graphic detail, Denny had no recollection of what happened next. What transpired, however, was recorded via a bird's-eye view by a passing news chopper, piloted by Bob Tur (now Zoey Tur). Millions across America watched in horror as

Antoine Miller opened the door of Denny's truck, allowing three other rioters to seize the driver by his long locks and yank him to the ground while he raided the cabin. These young men were thenceforth known as the "LA Four."

The same Henry Watson who ambushed Tarvin stamped down on Denny's head, holding him in place as another struck him in the gut with his foot. When Watson wandered off, two other unidentified rioters assaulted Denny. One of them, sporting a Malcolm X shirt, clobbered Denny in the skull with a five-pound oxygenator from Tarvin's truck. Denny tried to push himself off the asphalt, only to be struck in the head three more times with a tire iron. 19-year-old Damian Williams rounded off the gruesome ambush by swinging a thick slab of concrete at Denny's face.

Like Tarvin, Denny was temporarily stunned. Williams proceeded to showboat for the helicopter cameras with a touchdown dance, then flashed the gang sign of the Eight Tray Crips and giddily gestured at the mangled figure on the ground. Fellow gang member Anthony Brown (not included in the LA Four) spit the victim before sauntering off with Williams. Finally, Miller and homeless crack addict Gary Williams, the final member of the LA Four, stole Denny's wallet before fleeing the scene.

Denny miraculously regained consciousness moments later and clambered back into his truck, his shirt completely soaked with blood. He managed to start his truck and was a few feet down the road when four Good Samaritans who watched the onslaught on live TV came to his aid. All of Denny's rescuers were black. Lei Yuille hopped into the passenger's side and moved Denny close to her while Bobby Green, also a trucker, commanded the wheel. Titus Murphy dangled off the side of the vehicle, serving as Green's eyes since the windshield was completely shattered. Murphy's girlfriend, Terri Barnett, played escort by driving in front of the truck and guided them towards the hospital. Barnett later recounted the sinking feeling in her stomach when several police cruisers raced past them, ignoring the civilians desperately flagging them down.

The authorities' failure to stop these kinds of unprovoked attacks, along with the lack of other emergency responders, encouraged active rioters into wreaking more havoc and galvanized opportunists watching at home to join in on the rioting. Tur reported from the chopper, "In terms of police presence, there's none. Just terrible violence here. We up here in the air are not immune to it. People have been firing up at us from below. Fortunately, we're a small target in a big sky." The placards held by some spectators, also captured on tape, were blazoned with more violent slogans, such as "Kill Gates." People chanted, "All we want is to kill Gates. Kill Gates. Kill Gates. Kill that little red-necked m***********."

The first casualty of the riots was 23-year-old Arturo Miranda. Miranda was heading home from a soccer game with his nephew and a friend when he paused at a light in Green Meadows at 7:30 p.m. Out of nowhere, a blue car screeched to a stop next to him. The driver of the strange vehicle drew his pistol and fired one shot, hitting Miranda in the chest. Eight others were slain on the first day of the unrest.

10 minutes later, a "white-passing" Guatemalan construction worker named Fidel Lopez was yanked out of his pick-up by a separate mob, which included Damian Williams, at Florence and Normandie. The reprobates struck him in the head with a car stereo and beat him senseless. Not content with the humiliation their victim was already subjected to, Williams sprayed Lopez's face, limbs, and genitals with black paint, while accomplices drenched him in petrol and punched him some more. By the end of the beating, bloody flaps of flesh were hanging from Lopez's chin, and his ear had nearly been torn off. Reverend Bennie Newton, a black ex-convict-turned-minister, scurried over just before the rioters could set him aflame. Armed only with a Bible, Newton threw his body over Lopez's. "No more," the reverend roared. "This is

enough! Kill him and you'll have to kill me, too." The assailants cussed at Newton before moving away. By then, other members of the mob had already incinerated Lopez's truck, but not before bolting off with his tools and the $2,000 he was preparing to deposit in a bank.

Lopez's daughters and wife Coralia watched the attempted murder of her husband play out in their living room. She remembered how disturbed she was by the ruthless attack and the harrowing sympathy she felt for the poor man, only to later find out that the man was none other than her husband. Lopez later condemned the cops for their failure to protect him and the other riot victims. He said, "When they beat me, it was negligence on behalf of the police. Because of them, I nearly lost my life."

At 8:15 p.m., a black man named Dwight Taylor was gunned down by a passing car on West Martin Luther King Jr. Boulevard. His death was ruled accidental.

20 minutes later, officers from the Southwest Division surrounded a Latino man named Franklin Benavidez, who was reportedly in the midst of a gas station robbery. The cops claimed that the suspect had aimed his weapon at them, forcing them to discharge their weapons and hit him twice in the chest. Whether Benavidez was armed remains a matter of dispute since gunshot residue tests were never

conducted, but the cops were vindicated by the inquest verdict.

The riots rapidly spread to adjacent neighborhoods and cities in LA County like a fast-acting plague, affecting Pico-Union, South Central, and the Westside, as well as the intersection of North Alvarado and Beverly Boulevard near Filipinotown. They also spread to Compton, Inglewood, Hollywood, Lynwood, and Pasadena. A May 1992 *LA Times* article titled "Looting and Fires Ravage LA" painted a vivid picture of the pandemonium that had erupted in these parts: "Looters pilfered merchandise from mini-malls and swap meets throughout [the] combat zones...At some sites in the LA Basin, looting was so intense that gridlock snarled parking lots and streets as looters attempted to drive off with their goods. As they casually carted off everything from guns to diapers, some expressed fury over the King verdicts, but others went about their work in high spirits, seeming to enjoy the anarchy of the moment."

Ricky Bonilla's picture of people looting a clothing store

At 8:45 p.m., Mayor Bradley declared a local state of emergency and announced the deployment of 2,000 reserve soldiers from the National Guard. At 9:05 p.m., the exit ramps off the Harbor Freeway encompassing the Santa Monica Freeway junction to Century Boulevard were sealed, close to five hours after the start of the riots. A total of 110 exit ramps followed suit.

Civilians in these neighboring cities were also targeted in barbaric assaults, which occasionally ended in death. 15 minutes after the state of emergency was implemented, a powder-blue 1986 Ford Taurus belonging to a 33-year-old Mexican-American named Eduardo Vela stalled on Slauson Avenue in Ladera Heights. Vela's two friends, who were traveling with him, left him to guard the car as they searched for a payphone. Upon their return, they discovered Vela's lifeless corpse sprawled out on the ground with a bullet lodged in his bloodstained chest. About six miles east in South Central, a motorist came upon the body of a black 21-year-old nurse's assistant named Anthony Netherly, who was lying motionless on the street with a bleeding, gaping hole where his left eye used to be.

Shortly thereafter, the rioting in North Hollywood claimed its first soul. According to witnesses, some young black men were soliciting donations outside an apartment building, apparently to finance a campaign for the retrial of the officers involved in the King case. The men took offense at resident Victor Medina's $2 contribution and pressed him to cough up more money. Medina spurned their demands and attempted to make a break for it, but he was immobilized by a blow to the head. Medina's neighbor, Elias Rivera, inserted himself between the victim and his attackers, and he was also whacked on the head by the same hunk of wood, suffering a fatal fracturing of his skull. Rivera slipped into a coma and was ultimately taken off life support. 19-year-old Traville Craig was eventually sentenced to life in prison without the possibility of parole for Rivera's death.

At 11:00 p.m., Mayor Bradley returned to the podium to reassure the public that the city was collaborating with the Sheriff's Department and Highway Patrol, as well as local police and fire stations in the affected cities, to stop the violence as swiftly as possible. The mayhem was obviously far from over, but Bradley told people that "the situation [was] simmering down...[and] under control."

During the live broadcast of Bradley's media briefing, a horrendous head-on collision occurred in Mission Hills. A white resident named John Willers hastened over to help the motorists involved in the thunderous crash when, without warning, a car streaked past them and unloaded a hailstorm of bullets. Willers, struck in the heart, bled out on the spot. Half an hour later, a black resident of Gramercy Park named Elbert Wilkins died in similar fashion. He was leaning against one of his friends' cars, minding his own business, when he was shot in a drive-by shooting. Like Willers, a bullet pierced his chest and ruptured his aorta.

At 12:15 a.m. on April 30, a sunset-to-sunrise curfew was imposed by the city, effective immediately. The off-limits zone was bordered by Vernon Avenue on the north, the city limits on the east, Century Boulevard on the south, and Crenshaw Boulevard on the west, but the restricted area steadily expanded over the next few days. The sales of firearms and ammunition, along with the purchasing of non-vehicle-related petrol were also temporarily suspended under a city ordinance.

The inauguration of this directive coincided with the murder of Ira McCurry, a white employee of the LA County Parks and Recreation Department, in Watts. Reports revealed that McCurry had attempted to dissuade rioters from torching the store next to his residence. His pleas antagonized the arsonists, and the ensuing altercation concluded with one of the rioters shooting McCurry in the eye.

By the time the rioting had been going on for about eight hours, a suffocating canopy of impenetrable black smoke loomed over the heart of LA. The red-orange glows of the monstrous, sputtering flames interspersed across the otherwise pitch-dark neighborhoods seemed to be the only signs of life. Among the structures that had been reduced to ashes near ground zero of the riots were two auto-repair shops, a TV repair shop, and a gas station. The dining area of a church and the house of a pastor were also set alight.

Ricky Bonilla's picture of smoke over LA

Ricky Bonilla's picture of burned buildings in LA

Rick Taylor's picture of burned buildings in LA

The LA Fire Department received a staggering 1,000 calls on the first day. Soot-coated firefighters scrambled to extinguish roughly 120 blazes, mainly in liquor stores, strip-malls, mom-and-pop shops, other retail establishments, and various vehicles. Unfortunately, while firefighters and paramedics are often considered among the least controversial professions in the field of emergency services, they were targeted all the same. Passing firetrucks were arbitrarily shot at, and at least one firefighter sustained a gunshot wound. Some rioters charged at firefighters at work, swinging glinting axes, bats, planks, blocks of concrete, and other blunt objects, to prevent them from dousing said blazes. Police officers were therefore tasked with accompanying firefighters during their rounds. In the meantime, prank callers and ominous mischief-makers added to the tangling of emergency lines, the latter often dealing death threats to law enforcement. "I'm a member of the Eight Tray Gangster Crips," one anonymous caller barked. "Come this weekend, you'll know who we are."

The AME Church was among the first to convert its space to a shelter that housed residents displaced by fires, wounded victims unable to seek medical treatment in the packed hospitals, and those looking to escape the madness. The church also supplied food, water, and other essentials to the community, as the grocery stores and mini-marts in the area had been burned down, robbed, or had shuttered their doors.

By daybreak, the sobering reality of the previous night's frightful, devastating events, and more so the realization that the nightmare had yet to run its course, sunk in for many for the first time. That morning, all schools were closed, as were restaurants, retail shops, office buildings (excluding those in the emergency sector), courthouses, and other public spaces. Postal and bus services were terminated, and all professional sports matches scheduled for that day were postponed. The skies in affected regions were also cleared until further notice. A federal aviation representative explained the dangers that passing planes faced and their decision to reroute all flights to LAX: "We [wanted] to keep them high enough over the area of the looting to prevent small-arms fire from reaching those airplanes...The smoke from 1,000 fires grew so dense that air-traffic controllers could keep open only one runway at LAX."

At 8:00 a.m., 2,000 National Guardsmen assembled at the armories, but indecision and circumstances beyond the department's control delayed their deployment by four hours. The commanders' deliberation over the most practical ways to utilize the guardsmen lasted longer than originally planned because dealing with riots was an unusual task for the National Guard. Thus, they had to be primed on departmental procedures, and the arrival of necessary armaments from Camp Roberts also took longer than anticipated.

In the late afternoon, the city announced that hundreds of troops had been dispatched to all major flash-points across LA County. Police cruisers also made a show of coasting up and down the streets of the worst-hit neighborhoods with their rifles jutting out of their windows and sirens blaring. Many, however, were unimpressed by the "reinforcements" and dismissed them as useless theatrics and political grandstanding. The rioters continued to pave their paths of destruction more or less unabated.

KJLH, an all-music radio station based in Compton's Crenshaw Boulevard, switched off their usual soul tunes and adopted an all-talk hotline format for three days. In addition to feeding the public regular updates regarding the rioting, listeners were invited to call in so they could voice their concerns and air their grievances. Others called in to offer a play-by-play of the maelstrom of barbarity and turmoil outside their windows. From their vantage point, the station employees themselves had a hauntingly clear view of the streets. "We were prepared for people to be unhappy," Karen Slade recalled. "But we couldn't believe our eyes. People were beyond angry. They were crazy. It's like they lost their mind." Even through the airwaves, the distress of DJ "Rico" Reed, who hosted the show, was evident. Reed, at one point, stammered, "I'm just – excuse me. I'm just caught up in the emotion. There's so much going on outside the window."

Another critical chapter of the saga was the siege of Koreatown, or what the Koreans call "*Sa-i-gu,*" literally "April 29th." On that day, Tom's Liquor and the Pay-less Liquor and Deli were just two among the thousands of Korean-American shops that were obliterated by the rioters. *Radio Korea*, a major Korean-American station in LA, documented the disastrous scenes in this overlooked war-zone from start to finish. Much like their counterparts around the county, the hosts had trouble maintaining their composure at certain times and declined to tide their listeners over with false hope. Koreatown had been left to fend for itself, plain and simple. Initially, listeners were exhorted to board up the windows of their businesses as best they could, stay indoors with their front doors bolted shut, and pray. But as devout as they were, many Korean-Americans could not stomach the thought of looters stealing and burning their places. There would be no shortage of videos taken of young and middle-aged Korean men, clad in stereotypical 1990s fashion, posted up on rooftops and armed to the teeth with shotguns and automatic rifles, fully prepared to shoot down any rioter within five feet of their businesses. The so-called "Rooftop Koreans" have been immortalized in fan-made video tributes, niche memes, and even merchandise.

Kee Whanha, owner of the Hannam Supermarket chain, was one of the business owners who marshaled and mobilized a group of volunteers within the community to protect these endangered establishments. In an interview with *NPR,* Kee explained why he felt it imperative to form an impromptu defense force: "On Thursday morning, I expect something going to happen in Koreatown...I assembled my people, all the store owners, people who has a big rifle or hunting rifle, everything...We see that...[the next door owners had gone home]. Then the riot people came inside, and they steal everything. They put the gasoline, then they put the fire, so whole building's on fire...I know the owner of Radio Korea, so I brought my handgun and I put it on the table. I told him that we established Koreatown...I want to protect my business, as well as all other Korean businesses...It's like Wild West in old days, like there's nothing there. We are the only one left."

In the end, most Hannam branches succeeded in making a solid recovery, but tragedy still prevailed, for a security guard named Patrick Bettan lost his life. To make matters worse, Bettan had been fatally struck by friendly fire from the rooftop. Kee explained, "I was standing a few feet away, so I see that his body has fallen down on the ground, but I was so scared." Half of Bettan's head had been blown off. Kee draped a sheet of red packing paper over his employee's body and dialed for help at once. "We tried to call the fire department," said Kee. "Please help us. But nobody listen." By the time help finally arrived five hours later, rigor mortis had set in.

35-year-old Chang Lee was one of the able-bodied men who left his gas station unattended and lent himself to the frontline. Like many other young Koreans who surged forth, no questions asked, to protect their turf, Chang had never even held a gun, and yet he found himself holding one on that day. He kept one eye glued to the street below and the other to his portable TV. Like much of the rest of LA, the media was his lifeline, his only connection to what felt like the outside world. Suddenly, the aerial cameras panned to a flaming gas station. His mind fogged by fear and adrenaline, it took him a while to connect the dots, but then it dawned on him that the reason those gas pumps looked so familiar was because he handled them every day.

During a 2017 interview with *CNN*, Chang recounted the disenchantment and helplessness he felt when it finally registered that the cops weren't coming. "Nothing in my life indicated I was a secondary citizen until the LA Riots," said Chang. "The LAPD powers that be decided to protect the 'haves' and the Korean community did not have any political voice or power. They left us to burn."

Rooftops aside, armed Koreans scattered themselves across the ground floor. David Joo, who was working as a gun store manager at the time, received a frantic call from his boss Richard Park. The urgency in Park's voice rattled him. They needed him down at the jewelry shop (also owned by Park) right away, and there was no time for details, much less pleasantries. "We're having a gun fight here," Park blurted. "Can you just come over and help us?"

Joo geared up and made a beeline for Park's location. He recalled the fleeting moment of relief that washed over him when he spotted a police car with four uniformed occupants. It had taken them long enough, but they were there, and now all would be well, or so he thought. The instant a round of gunfire rang out, the squad car drove off. Stranded, Joo and his fellow defenders decided to take matters into their own hands and squared off with the rioters, some of whom were also armed. Joo was one of the more memorable stars, so to speak, of those popular Rooftop Koreans highlight reels. A bespectacled man with a tight crew-cut and a khaki vest can be seen sprinting down the street with his pistol raised and signaling the rioters to back off. In another shot, he can be seen leaning with his back pressed up against a pillar, and in another, he blasts away one-handed at a screeching car, his free arm swinging. "I didn't hesitate to shoot them," said Joo. "Otherwise, I could have got shot...Even though you're scared, you don't have much option. You have to fight."

Some Korean business owners fought back without firearms. Another harrowing clip shows a Korean woman with salt-streaked hair and a white sweater blackened with dirt positioned where her door, or possibly wall, once stood. She splayed out her arms and legs, glaring down at the mob of would-be looters with widened, unblinking eyes. "Don't you dare set a fire!" she screamed. "Get out! I'm closed. This is America! Get out!"

By the end of the rioting, Koreatown was littered with bodies, many of which were only unearthed from the rubble several days later. There was the burnt body of William Ross, a 25-year-old black man, who was found in the fetal position under a desk in the back office of a grocery store that had been raided and firebombed. The body of 20-year-old Nissar Mustafa was only found amongst the debris in the J.J. Newberry discount store four months later.

Yet another name on the lengthy list of unnecessary deaths was 18-year-old "Edward" Lee Jaesong. The teenager had felt compelled to defend Koreatown with his brethren, and he did precisely that, against his mother's wishes. At 10:00 p.m., Lee linked up with the other guards outside a Korean canteen called *Wonsan Myeonok*. Armed black looters, the others told Lee, had infiltrated the rooftop. A shootout inevitably ensued, and Lee was caught in the crossfire.

A few hours later, Lee's mother heard a radio report about a dead body that had been discovered on a sidewalk near 3rd Street and Hobart Boulevard. The next morning, she came across the same story on a Korean newspaper, but this one came with a photograph taken by Kang

Hyungwon of the *LA Times*. There he was in the foreground, lying limp on the concrete with an outstretched arm. In the background was a group of policemen, flashlights and notepads in hand, hunched over as they questioned three other men who had also suffered gunshot wounds.

Lee's mother recalled how puzzled she was by the black shirt he had on in the photograph, as she distinctly remembered the white shirt he was wearing that day. She later realized that the black was "my son's blood." Then came the second depressing revelation: there were no black looters on that roof. The man who pulled the trigger was another Korean-American resident who, like Lee, only wanted to protect the place.

In all, 26 people were killed during the second day of rioting. Howard Epstein was shot in the temple as he was driving down Slauson Avenue, and his Ford Thunderbird zigzagged down the road and slammed into a tree. Rioters swarmed the smoking vehicle immediately and rabidly rifled through the interior with the bleeding Epstein still strapped into his seat. *LA Fire* contributor Jim Crogan later wrote, "The crowd's hostility was so intense, police towed the car with the body still inside."

Not all those who died were killed by rioters. 17-year-old Deandre Harrison was shot by the police in South

Central, and 15-year-old Mark Garcia, who was allegedly involved in a jewelry heist, suffered a gunshot in the chest shortly after his getaway car crashed. Hector Castro was simply walking down the street when he was shot in the spine by a National Guardsman in East Hollywood. His death was ruled accidental, and ultimately no charges were filed.

At 6:35 p.m., 15 black youths in Long Beach pulled Matthew Haines and his nephew off his motorbike and mugged them. Haines, who was headed downtown to pick up a black friend whose van had broken down, attempted to defuse the situation by assuring his assailants that they were on the "same side." The rioters responded by beating him and shooting him in the back of the head. His nephew survived. Three of the attackers were convicted of assault and conspiracy to commit burglary, and they would go on to serve 18 years between them.

African-American business owners hung up signs with the words "Black-Owned" printed in bold in the hopes that the rioters, who were supposedly acting out to protest discrimination and the justice system, would leave their establishments alone. At one plaza, the only store that survived the looting and arson attacks had a "Black-Owned" placard, scrawled in white shoe polish, taped to the front window. In an amateur video shot by a sympathetic civilian, a middle-aged African-American gentleman in a pastel-yellow shirt and gray cap is seen remonstrating with rioters on the street, his raspy voice strained with powerful emotion. "Don't destroy my stuff," he cried, pounding the air in anguish. "Don't burn down my [inaudible]. I worked too hard for this! It's not right...what you all doing! I came from the ghetto, too. Same as all of you kids...Why steal my computer? I'm trying to make it."

Similarly, some shopkeepers, at their wit's end, tried to appeal to the looters by drawing attention to their ethnic backgrounds. A Filipino man identified only as "Rommel" described how he persuaded a group of Hispanic looters to spare his father's food market: "We told them, 'We're the same color. Why should you hit us?' We begged, and they just left."

However, not all minority businesses were so fortunate. Several people who called in to *KJLH* were heartbroken black entrepreneurs who had lost their precious ventures – many of them multi-generational family businesses – overnight. Another black business owner who fell victim to looters was interviewed by an *Inside Edition* camera crew. "What can we do?" said the man as looters milled in and out of his boutique with stacks of clothes piled higher than their heads, completely unbothered by the media presence. "It makes you mad, naturally, 'cause you work hard to build something up, and your own people destroy it...At this point, I don't think anyone knows what they're after. I think they're just caught up in the moment."

John Mitchell, a reporter of the *LA Times*, came to the aid of Tam Tran, who had been ambushed by rioters at Florence and Normandie. After rioters hurled a brick into Tam Tran's car, slicing her cheek open, and bashed in the other windows, the woman exited her car in a daze and collapsed to her knees. When Mitchell saw the horde closing in on Tran, he elbowed past them, ushered her towards his car, and drove her to Daniel Freeman Hospital.

Hongkongese bookkeeper Sai-Choi Choi, who was yanked out of his Ford Fiesta at Florence and Normandie, and brutally beaten and robbed by multiple black rioters, was saved by a black off-duty firefighter named Donald Jones. Jones took Choi to Fire Station 57, where he called for help, and waited with him until the paramedics came.

Raul Aguilar, a native of Belize, was struck by a crowbar and pummeled by a flurry of fists by a throng of youths. Somewhat mercifully, Aguilar had already been knocked out cold when his assailants decided to run over his leg, crushing the entire limb. James Henry, who only arrived after the assault, darted off his porch into the street and carried Aguilar to the sidewalk, lest he be flattened by the cars hurtling back and forth. Henry flagged down a

SWAT van, and when met with reluctance, he physically placed Aguilar's body on the floor between the seats. The SWAT crew eventually caved in and drove Aguilar to the emergency room.

At 11:59 p.m., Mayor Bradley notified the public that the city had filed a request for 4,000 additional National Guardsmen, and a glimmer of hope flickered on May 1, the third day of the riots. Over 1,000 Korean-Americans gathered at Western Avenue and Wilshire Boulevard for a peace march. At 2:45 p.m., 45 minutes after Pomona was placed on lockdown, Rodney King himself appeared on television screens. Standing outside of his attorney's office in Beverly Hills, a tearful King stepped forward and spoke into the cluster of microphones thrust into his face. "I just wanna say," King started, his muted voice trembling. "Can we get along? Can we all get along? Can we stop making it horrible for the older people and the kids?...It's just not right. It's not right, and it's not gonna change anything. We'll get our justice. They won the battle, but they haven't won the war...We've got to quit...Those people will never go home to their families again...We're all stuck here for a while. Let's try and work it out."

On the morning of the May 2, the arraignment of 6,000 alleged rioters who had been arrested so far commenced. At 11:00 that morning, Koreatown hosted another peace rally, with this one attended by 30,000 individuals of all races and ages. By the day's end, the mayhem had gone from an unbridled, city-wide inferno to more manageable pockets of rioting.

Reverend Jesse Jackson arrived in LA on the fifth day. The minister was introduced to Koreatown leaders and merchants, and the two parties engaged in discourse that aimed to mend the bridges between the African-American and Korean-American communities. Afterwards, the reverend delivered sermons at various churches across the county, including the chiefly white episcopal church in Pasadena and the predominantly black Praises of Zion Baptist Church in South Central. He attempted to pacify seething protesters and consoled somber crowds outside *KJLH* and what remained of the Greenmead Post Office, and he offered prayers to riot victims at an Inglewood hospital.

Jackson was criticized for some of the analogies he drew during his speech, some of which were considered insensitive and irrelevant. At one point, he rambled about the struggles of a Japanese-American gold-winning Olympian to his Korean-American crowd. Some critics accused him of exploiting the pain of struggling communities to promote a political campaign. That said, his long-winded speeches were laced with threads of predictable, but valuable wisdom. "We must go from pain to partnership, not pain to polarization," Jackson declared. "Keep hope alive, rebuild America."

Jackson

By the late afternoon of May 3, 6,500 National Guardsmen, 1,100 Marines, and 600 military personnel were spread out across Los Angeles. Excluding the handfuls of looters still scavenging around the skeletons of wreckages, most of the rioters had vacated the streets, and the ghost towns were a chilling encapsulation of the riots' consequences. Mountains of rubble, glass, and unidentifiable debris still exhaling plumes of smoke replaced longstanding corner stores. Ash rained down on the streets, where charred vehicles and car parts, chunks of concrete, mounds of bricks, and spray-paint bottles lay strewn about. Shops and restaurants lucky enough to escape, and those that survived the blazes, were left with blackened signs, upturned furniture, toppled shelves, and thousands of dollars' worth of missing or wasted merchandise.

Commercial establishments weren't the only ones laid to waste. The rampage also claimed a number of irreplaceable historical monuments and artifacts, among them the Young Market Building and all the antique marble and mosaics it housed. Other casualties included the Bullocks Wilshire and a building belonging to 100 Black Men of America, a civic organization dedicated to empowering black children and teenagers.

That same day, Mayor Bradley announced that the curfew would be lifted the following day. The Harbor Freeway off-ramps were reopened, and select buses were allowed to restart their routes. Meanwhile, an additional 6,345 were arrested for their alleged involvement in the rioting.

At 7:40 p.m., Victor Rivas was shot dead by a National Guardsman in the Rampart area of Pico-Union. Rivas, who was breaching curfew, had reportedly struck one of the guardsmen with his 1974 Datsun, prompting the soldiers to open fire 14 times. Rivas was the last casualty of the LA riots.

Children returned to school, and adults headed to work on the morning of May 4. Police officers and state soldiers continued to patrol the streets, but for the first time that week, LA had achieved a sense of normalcy. With that, the 1992 LA Riots technically ended. Still ahead, however, was a long and winding road of rebuilding, dialogue, and healing.

63 people lost their lives in the LA Riots, and 23 of those deaths remain unsolved to this day. Of the thousands injured, 2,383 were hospitalized, with many suffering life-altering injuries and lasting psychological trauma. At least 3,600 individual fires were ignited within the five days, and the overall damages amounted to over $1 billion. Over 2,200 Korean-owned establishments had been ransacked, suffering irreparable damages or complete destruction. In all, the damages sustained in Koreatown alone accounted for $400 million.

The rebuilding of the damaged parts of Los Angeles unified the county's multicultural residents in the following months. Community leaders and residents formed voluntary clean-up crews, lightening the grueling workload of the city-employed custodians. A representative of Senator Diane Watson's office, one of the organizers in South Central, remarked, "The ones who were doing the burning [and] the looting are not here today. These are the ones who want to reclaim the community. We are all equals today. Hopefully, this will be a trend." Karen Slade of *KJLH* praised Compton's residents for their indomitable spirits. "One lady came out, and she had some of the neighborhood kids," Slade recalled. "And she got them brooms and everybody was sweeping. They were cleaning up Crenshaw; I had never seen it before!"

Numerous organizations and public figures also contributed to the cause. The Saigu and Korean Churches for Community Development, as well as Operation Hope, raised and donated millions towards rebuilding and renovations, boosting the local economy. The Rebuild LA Program pledged to create 74,000 jobs with their $6 billion contribution. Michael Jackson personally gifted $1.25 million to establish a foundation devoted to the medical treatment and mental health counseling of inner-city children. Actor and activist Edward James Olmos rolled up his sleeves and got his hands dirty, joining volunteer sweepers in the streets.

On October 21, 1991, the Webster Commission, spearheaded by FBI Director William Webster, presented its findings to the Board of Police Commissioners. The task force, which had been established to investigate the department's agonizingly slow response to the crisis, determined that both the LAPD and City Hall leaders were to blame for the fiasco. The following recommendations were issued to both parties, whose lack of preparation and communication were underscored by the task force:

"1. The LAPD should place a greater emphasis on basic patrol duties by reallocating police officers away from special units and toward patrol assignments.

2. Both the LAPD and the City of LA should devote more resources to emergency response planning and training.

3. The city should overhaul its emergency operations center and emergency communications system to better coordinate emergency response procedures."

Gates resigned and retired from law enforcement and the public eye on June 28, 1992. This came 25 days after the passage of Charter Amendment F, the statute on police reform that Gates had so vehemently opposed.

On December 7, Damian Williams was sentenced to 10 years in prison for his involvement in the aggravated assaults on Reginald Denny and four other civilians at

Florence and Normandie. Williams was released after four years, but he was sent back to prison after he murdered a drug dealer in 2000, for which he received a sentence of 46 years to life.

Gary Williams, who pleaded guilty, was incarcerated for three years. Miller received 27 months probation, and he was shot and killed in a Hollywood nightclub in 2005. As for Watson, he was convicted of misdemeanor assault and was sentenced to time served for the one year and five months he spent behind bars prior to the closing of his case. Watson also apologized to and made peace with Denny on the *Phil Donahue* show.

Much to the delight of the public, the four officers were tried by a federal court. On April 17, 1993, Koon and Powell were found guilty of violating Rodney King's civil rights, while Briseno and Wind were both acquitted. On August 3, a jury awarded King $3.8 million in damages in a lawsuit he filed against the city of LA, plus $1.7 million to cover attorney fees. The next day, Koon and Powell were each sentenced to 30 months in prison, sentences that were criticized by many for being too light.

Rodney King's body was discovered at the bottom of his swimming pool on June 17, 2012. The 47-year-old had battled with alcoholism for the rest of his life. The year of his death, he had been making solid progress with his sobriety and was engaged to Cynthia Kelley, who served as one of the jurors in King's civil suit against the city. According to Kelley, King had suffered a relapse and had been "drinking and smoking weed all day" on the day of his death.

Rodney King remains a household name in America, and the 1992 LA Riots have continued to be a cultural touchstone, whether described in songs by artists of various genres or cited by activists and protesters who have complained that there is plenty of work left to do. Recently, an *NPR* investigation found that 135 unarmed black civilians had been killed by police since 2015. Cheryl Thompson of *NPR* noted, "For at least 15 of the officers...the shootings were not their first – or their last...They have been involved in two – sometimes three or more – shootings, often deadly and without consequences...More than two dozen officers have racked up citizen complaints or use-of-force incidents. A Fort Lauderdale officer had 82 reviews over use-of-force incidents, but was never found in violation."

Online Resources

Other books about 20th century history by Charles River Editors

Other books about the LA riots on Amazon

Further Reading

Banks, S. (2020). *How the LA Riots Changed Everything and Nothing*. https://www.aetv.com/specials/l-a-burning-the-riots-25-years-later/articles/the-l-a-riots-25-years-later-what-have-we-learned.

Barragan, B., Chandler, J., & Kudler, A. G. (2020, May 1). *Mapping the 1992 LA Uprising.* https://la.curbed.com/maps/1992-los-angeles-riots-rodney-king-map.

Baum, D. (2016, April). *Legalize It All.* https://harpers.org/archive/2016/04/legalize-it-all/.

Bermudez, E. (2012, April 29). *Fading memories at Florence and Normandie.* https://www.latimes.com/nation/la-xpm-2012-apr-29-la-me-riot-fading-memories-20120429-story.html.

Boyer, E. J., & Ford, A. (1992, May 8). *Black-Owned Businesses Pay a Heavy Price.* https://www.latimes.com/archives/la-xpm-1992-05-08-mn-1884-story.html.

Braxton, G., & Newton, J. (1992, March 1). *From the Archives: Looting and fires ravage L.A.: 25 dead, 572 injured; 1,000 blazes reported.* https://www.latimes.com/local/california/la-me-looting-and-fires-ravage-la-19920501-story.html.

Brodsky, M. (2018, March 25). *OLE MISS RIOT (1962)*. https://www.blackpast.org/african-american-history/ole-miss-riot-1962/.

Bukszpan, D. (2011, February 1). *America's Most Destructive Riots of All Time*. https://www.cnbc.com/2011/02/01/Americas-Most-Destructive-Riots-of-All-Time.html.

Buncombe, A. (2020, May 4). *LA riots: Rioter in infamous footage of trucker being pulled from vehicle says 'nothing has changed' since 1992*. https://www.independent.co.uk/news/world/americas/la-riots-anniversary-eyewitness-rioter-truck-henry-keith-watson-rodney-king-a9496066.html.

Cannon, L. (1992, April 30). *National Guard Called to Stem Violence After L.A. Officers' Acquittal in Beating*. https://www.washingtonpost.com/wp-srv/national/longterm/lariots/stories/origverdict.htm.

Cannon, L. (1992, May 10). *WHEN THIN BLUE LINE RETREATED, L.A. RIOT WENT OUT OF CONTROL*. https://www.washingtonpost.com/archive/politics/1992/05/10/when-thin-blue-line-retreated-la-riot-went-out-of-control/2ccf3e5c-c03b-4d82-bce1-0ea43be30cd3/?utm_term=.4da428dd604c.

Cannon, L. (1998, January 26). *WORLDS COLLIDE AT FLORENCE AND NORMANDIE.* https://www.washingtonpost.com/archive/politics/1998/01/26/worlds-collide-at-florence-and-normandie/5bfed605-0da1-4bfd-b69f-bc1cef8b7cc8/.

Chae, A. J. (2002, December 1). *To Be Almost Like White: The Case of Soon Ja Du* . https://digitalcommons.unomaha.edu/cgi/viewcontent.cgi?article=1456&context=studentwork.

Chang, A. (2020, June 1). *The History Of Protests In Los Angeles: What Has Changed Since The Rodney King Riots*. https://www.npr.org/2020/06/01/867256404/the-history-of-protests-in-los-angeles-what-has-changed-since-the-rodney-king-ri.

Constante, A. (2017, April 25). *25 Years After LA Riots, Koreatown Finds Strength in 'Saigu' Legacy.* https://www.nbcnews.com/news/asian-america/25-years-after-la-riots-koreatown-finds-strength-saigu-legacy-n749081.

Corwin, M. (1992, May 6). *RIOT AFTERMATH : Man With a Mission : Jesse Jackson Follows Crises Around the Globe--and the Media Follow Him.* https://www.latimes.com/archives/la-xpm-1992-05-06-mn-1260-story.html.

Crogan, J. (2002, May 2). *The L.A. 53.*
https://www.lafire.com/famous_fires/1992-0429_LA-
Riots/LAWEEKLY-2002-0426/2002-
0426_laweekly_TheLA53_Crogan.htm.

Dazio, S. (2021, April 21). *Flashpoint of 1992 LA riots
becomes a place of celebration.*
https://apnews.com/article/george-floyd-death-of-george-
floyd-riots-f00f7bb9fe794c8dfbacc75827ea8050.

Editors, A. P. (2012, April 25). *Major players in the
1992 Los Angeles riot.*
https://www.sandiegouniontribune.com/sdut-major-
players-in-the-1992-los-angeles-riot-2012apr25-
story.html.

Editors, A. P. (2017, April 27). *Rodney King riot:
Timeline of key events.*
https://apnews.com/article/fa4d04d8281443fc8db0e27d6b
e52081.

Editors, A. P. (2017, April 29). *7 key moments from 1992
LA riots.* https://abc7.com/los-angeles-riots-la-1992-
rodney-king/1921781/.

Editors, A. P. (2020, May 30). *A Timeline of US Race
Riots Since 1965.* https://www.voanews.com/usa/timeline-
us-race-riots-1965.

Editors, B. B. (2021, June 25). *George Floyd murder: Derek Chauvin sentenced to over 22 years.* https://www.bbc.com/news/world-us-canada-57618356.

Editors, B. C. (2014, April 2). *Rodney King.* https://www.biography.com/crime-figure/rodney-king.

Editors, C. B. (2012, June 17). *Leaders React To Rodney King's Death.* https://losangeles.cbslocal.com/2012/06/17/leaders-react-to-news-of-rodney-kings-death/.

Editors, C. L. (1974, October 3). *Edward Garner Shot and Killed by Memphis Police; Case Reaches Supreme Court.* https://todayinclh.com/?event=edward-garner-shot-and-killed-case-reaches-supreme-court.

Editors, C. N. (2012, June 18). *Rodney King dead at 47.* https://edition.cnn.com/2012/06/17/us/obit-rodney-king/index.html.

Editors, D. N. (1992, April 24). *SEQUESTERED JURY STARTS DELIBERATIONS IN KING ASSAULT TRIAL.* https://www.deseret.com/1992/4/24/18980549/sequestered-jury-starts-deliberations-in-king-assault-trial.

Editors, F. L. (2020). *PEOPLE of the State of California, Petitioner, v. SUPERIOR COURT of Los Angeles County, Respondent. SOON JA DU, Real Party in*

Interest. https://caselaw.findlaw.com/ca-court-of-appeal/1769555.html.

Editors, H. C. (2009, December 16). *Haymarket Riot*. https://www.history.com/topics/19th-century/haymarket-riot.

Editors, H. C. (2019, December 17). *War on Drugs*. https://www.history.com/topics/crime/the-war-on-drugs.

Editors, H. C. (2021, April 20). *Los Angeles Riots*. https://www.history.com/topics/1990s/the-los-angeles-riots.

Editors, H. C. (2021, April 27). *Riots erupt in Los Angeles after police officers are acquitted in Rodney King trial*. https://www.history.com/this-day-in-history/riots-erupt-in-los-angeles.

Editors, H. C. (2021, March 2). *LAPD officers beat Rodney King on camera*. https://www.history.com/this-day-in-history/police-brutality-caught-on-video.

Editors, H. C. (2021, May 17). *Civil Rights Movement*. https://www.history.com/topics/black-history/civil-rights-movement.

Editors, L. T. (2012, April 25). *Deaths during the L.A. riots*. https://spreadsheets.latimes.com/la-riots-deaths/.

Editors, L. T. (2017, April 26). *The L.A. Riots: 25 years later.* https://www.independent.co.uk/news/world/americas/la-riots-anniversary-eyewitness-rioter-truck-henry-keith-watson-rodney-king-a9496066.html.

Editors, M. (2021, April 11). *Latasha Harlins: The 15-Year-Old Murdered Over Orange Juice.* https://medium.com/crimebeat/latasha-harlins-the-15-year-old-murdered-over-orange-juice-7cdee60c3834.

Editors, N. P. (2012, April 13). *Colleagues Recall L.A. Riots Unfolding Like 'A Movie'.* https://www.npr.org/2012/04/13/150509967/colleagues-recall-l-a-riots-unfolding-like-a-movie.

Editors, N. P. (2012, April 27). *Korean Store Owner On Arming Himself For Riots.* https://www.npr.org/2012/04/27/151526930/korean-store-owner-on-arming-himself-for-riots.

Editors, N. Y. (1982, May 13). *COAST POLICE CHIEF ACCUSED OF RACISM.* https://www.nytimes.com/1982/05/13/us/coast-police-chief-accused-of-racism.html.

Editors, N. Z. (2002, April 30). *Fear and hatred linger 10 years after LA riots.* https://www.nzherald.co.nz/world/fear-and-hatred-linger-

10-years-after-la-
riots/CBEXQ7CASHTHBD3RC2CLS5RV54/.

Editors, O. A. (2008). *Los Angeles Webster Commission records*.
https://oac.cdlib.org/findaid/ark:/13030/kt0580335h/admin/.

Editors, T. B. (1992, May 13). *4 arrested in beating of truck driver in L.A.*
https://www.tampabay.com/archive/1992/05/13/4-arrested-in-beating-of-truck-driver-in-l-a/.

Editors, U. D. (1993). *Bureau of Justice Statistics Bulletin 1992*. https://bjs.ojp.gov/content/pub/pdf/ji92.pdf.

Editors, U. D. (1994). *Bureau of Justice Statistics - Correctional Populations in the US*.
https://www.ojp.gov/pdffiles1/Digitization/153849NCJRS.pdf.

Flores, J. (2019, October 8). *Do liquor stores like Tom's still have a place in South LA?*
https://la.curbed.com/2019/10/8/20897705/toms-liquor-stores-south-la.

Francis, E., & Patria, M. (2017, April 29). *'Let It Fall': Jung Hui Lee, whose son was killed during the LA uprising, in her own words.*

https://abcnews.go.com/Entertainment/fall-jung-hui-lee-son-killed-la-uprising/story?id=46715436.

Fuchs, C. (2017, April 25). *Communities Work to Build Understanding 25 Years After LA Riots.* https://www.nbcnews.com/news/asian-america/communities-work-build-understanding-25-years-after-la-riots-n748591.

Gallegos, E. G. (2012, June 17). *Rodney King's Fiancée: He Was Drinking All Yesterday.* https://laist.com/news/rodney-kings-fiancee-says-he-was-dr.

Garrison, A. H. (2020, June 12). *Your View: A history of white race riots in America.* https://www.mcall.com/opinion/mc-opi-unrest-america-garrison-20200612-6xczgrlphjgtjiosfde2mdrvbe-story.html.

Greene, R. (1993, May 26). *Riot Victim Pushes for a Monument to Good Samaritans : Memorial: Raul Aguilar was severely beaten during last year's violence. Now recovered, he wants the city to pay tribute to the people who rescued him from attackers.* https://www.latimes.com/archives/la-xpm-1993-05-26-ga-39960-story.html.

Holguin, R., & Lee, J. H. (1991, June 18). *Boycott of Store Where Man Was Killed Is Urged : Racial tensions: The African-American was slain while allegedly trying to rob the market owned by a Korean-American.* https://www.latimes.com/archives/la-xpm-1991-06-18-me-837-story.html.

Jennings, A. (2017, April 26). *He tried to cool a city's anger, only to watch helplessly as it burned during the 1992 riots.* https://www.latimes.com/local/lanow/la-me-riots-first-hours-ame-20170426-story.html.

King, C. I. (2020, June 19). *Opinion: America has always known about systemic police brutality. Will we finally do something about it?* https://www.washingtonpost.com/opinions/this-country-has-always-known-about-systemic-police-brutality-will-we-finally-do-something-about-it/2020/06/19/fcf0b246-b1a8-11ea-8f56-63f38c990077_story.html.

Kopetman, R., & Krikorian, G. (1992, May 4). *A MURDER MARKED BY IRONY.* https://www.washingtonpost.com/archive/politics/1992/05/04/a-murder-marked-by-irony/bba276a1-1ba9-477e-b377-ba2c29955276/.

Kuettner, A. (1962, October 1). *Ole Miss enrolls Meredith after riots kill 2, injure 75.*

https://www.upi.com/Archives/1962/10/01/Ole-Miss-enrolls-Meredith-after-riots-kill-2-injure-75/4258814340955/.

Lah, K. (2017, April 29). *The LA riots were a rude awakening for Korean-Americans.* https://edition.cnn.com/2017/04/28/us/la-riots-korean-americans/index.html.

Leibowitz, E. (2015, April 29). *Remembering the View from Florence and Normandie During the Riots of '92.* https://www.lamag.com/citythinkblog/remembering-the-view-from-florence-and-normandie-during-the-1992-riots-of-92/.

Lewis, F. (2020, December 16). *Black History Timeline: 1990–1999.* https://www.thoughtco.com/african-american-history-timeline-1990-1999-45447.

Lockridge, D. (2012, April 29). *A look back at the LA Race Riots, a trucker beating and the heroes who came to his aid.* https://www.truckinginfo.com/158725/a-look-back-at-the-la-race-riots-a-trucker-beating-and-the-heroes-who-came-to-hi.

Lopez, S. (2012, May 6). *The forgotten victim from Florence and Normandie.* https://www.latimes.com/local/la-xpm-2012-may-06-la-me-0506-lopez-riot-20120506-story.html.

Martin, D. (2013, June 30). *Rena Price is Dead at 97; Catalyst for the Watts Riots.* https://www.nytimes.com/2013/06/30/us/rena-price-is-dead-at-97-catalyst-for-the-watts-riots.html.

Miranda, C. A. (2017, April 27). *Of the 63 people killed during '92 riots, 23 deaths remain unsolved — artist Jeff Beall is mapping where they fell.* https://www.latimes.com/entertainment/arts/miranda/la-et-cam-la-riots-jeff-beall-los-angeles-uprising-20170427-htmlstory.html.

Mitchell, J. (1992, April 30). '*No One Else Made a Move to Help.*' https://www.latimes.com/archives/la-xpm-1992-04-30-mn-1924-story.html.

Monroe, R. (2013, September 29). *Common Ground: Brenda Stevenson's "The Contested Murder of Latasha Harlins."* https://lareviewofbooks.org/article/common-ground-brenda-stevensons-the-contested-murder-of-latasha-harlins/.

Morris, R. (2012, April 29). *LA riots: How 1992 changed the police.* https://www.bbc.com/news/world-us-canada-17878180.

Mrozek, T. (1993, September 28). *Man Convicted in Riot-Related Valley Murder : Courts: Traville Craig, 20, will get life in prison without possibility of parole for*

robbery victim's death. He will be sentenced Oct. 25.
https://www.latimes.com/archives/la-xpm-1993-09-28-
me-39913-story.html.

Mydans, S. (1991, October 6). *Shooting Puts Focus on
Korean-Black Frictions in Los Angeles.*
https://www.nytimes.com/1991/10/06/us/shooting-puts-
focus-on-korean-black-frictions-in-los-angeles.html.

Mydans, S. (1992, April 30). *THE POLICE VERDICT;
Los Angeles Policemen Acquitted in Taped Beating.*
https://archive.nytimes.com/www.nytimes.com/books/98/
02/08/home/rodney-verdict.html.

Naftali, T. (2019, July 31). *Ronald Reagan's Long-
Hidden Racist Conversation With Richard Nixon.*
https://www.theatlantic.com/ideas/archive/2019/07/ronald
-reagans-racist-conversation-richard-nixon/595102/.

Neal, E. (2021, April 20). *A history of police violence in
America.* https://stacker.com/stories/4365/history-police-
violence-america.

Philips, D. (2021, February 26). *Before George Floyd
and Breonna Taylor, There Was Latasha Harlins.*
https://www.nbclosangeles.com/news/national-
international/latasha-harlins-mural-los-angeles-
riots/2537429/.

Poon, L., & Patino, M. (2020, June 10). *CityLab University: A Timeline of U.S. Police Protests.* https://www.bloomberg.com/news/articles/2020-06-09/a-history-of-protests-against-police-brutality.

Raphael, S. (2020, September 21). *Where Is Soon Ja Du Now? She Fatally Shot Latasha Harlins in 1991.* https://www.distractify.com/p/soon-ja-du-now.

Ross, J. (2020, January 23). *How police justify shootings: The 1974 killing of an unarmed teen set a standard.* https://www.nbcnews.com/news/nbcblk/officer-killed-unarmed-teen-1974-it-changed-how-police-justify-n1120611.

Rothman, L. (2015, August 11). *50 Years After Watts: The Causes of a Riot.* https://time.com/3974595/watts-riot-1965-history/.

Rutten, T. (1991, June 21). *Unity Also a Victim of Shootings.* https://www.latimes.com/archives/la-xpm-1991-06-21-vw-935-story.html.

Sagahan, L., & Schwada, J. (1992, June 3). *Measure to Reform LAPD Wins Decisively.* https://www.latimes.com/archives/la-xpm-1992-06-03-mn-641-story.html.

Sahagun, L. (1991, August 31). *Blacks Won't End Korean Store Boycott.*

https://www.newspapers.com/clip/7449251/83191-blacks-wont-end-korean/.

Sastry, A., & Bates, K. G. (2017, April 26). *When LA Erupted In Anger: A Look Back At The Rodney King Riots*. https://www.npr.org/2017/04/26/524744989/when-la-erupted-in-anger-a-look-back-at-the-rodney-king-riots.

Stevenson, B. E. (2019). *LATASHA HARLINS, SOON JA DU, AND JOYCE KARLIN: A CASE STUDY OF MULTICULTURAL FEMALE VIOLENCE AND JUSTICE ON THE URBAN FRONTIER*. https://www.journals.uchicago.edu/doi/pdfplus/10.2307/4134098.

Sugrue, T. J. (2020, June 12). *2020 is not 1968: To understand today's protests, you must look further back*. https://www.nationalgeographic.com/history/article/2020-not-1968.

Sugrue, T. J. (Ed.). (2002, March 10). *Terror in the Streets*. https://www.washingtonpost.com/archive/entertainment/books/2002/03/10/terror-in-the-streets/499f11e8-b7ef-45af-ae4f-3163748991b6/.

Thompson, C. W. (2021, January 25). *Fatal Police Shootings Of Unarmed Black People Reveal Troubling Patterns*.

https://www.npr.org/2021/01/25/956177021/fatal-police-shootings-of-unarmed-black-people-reveal-troubling-patterns.

Whitman, D. (1993, May 23). *The Untold Story of the LA Riot*. https://www.usnews.com/news/articles/1993/05/23/the-untold-story-of-the-la-riot.

Wong, B. (2020, June 11). *The Real, Tragic Story Behind That 'Roof Korean' Meme You May Have Seen.* https://www.huffpost.com/entry/roof-koreans-meme-know-real-story_n_5ee110a1c5b6d5bafa5604f3.

Worthington, R. (1993, March 30). *PATROL OFFICER SAYS SHE DIDN'T AID KING FOR FEAR OF HECKLING.* https://www.chicagotribune.com/news/ct-xpm-1993-03-30-9303300047-story.html.

Yamato, J. (2017, April 28). *'Look what happens when we don't talk to each other': Korean American filmmakers' L.A. riots stories.* https://www.latimes.com/entertainment/movies/la-et-mn-la-riots-korean-american-filmmakers-20170428-htmlstory.html.

Free Books by Charles River Editors

We have brand new titles available for free most days of the week. To see which of our titles are currently free, click on this link.

Discounted Books by Charles River Editors

We have titles at a discount price of just 99 cents everyday. To see which of our titles are currently 99 cents, click on this link.